So You Want to Be a Waiter/Waitress, Huh!

By Mr. Clarence E Palmer Sr

DORRANCE
PUBLISHING CO
EST. 1920
PITTSBURGH, PENNSYLVANIA 15238

Dorrance Publishing Co
585 Alpha Drive
Suite 103
Pittsburgh, PA 15238
Visit our website at *www.dorrancebookstore.com*

ISBN: 978-1-4809-8423-3
eISBN: 978-1-4809-8442-4

So You Want to Be a Waiter/Waitress, Huh!

Contents

So, You Want to Be a Waiter/Waitress, Huh!

Okay, let's get started. This information that you are receiving cannot, nor will not, be taught in nobody's classroom. Lucky you, then there was Clarence. First, to have been a waiter in America, you were considered a low, unacceptable individual and most likely black. As slavery ended, society grew and time moved on, opening a restaurant was the American dream, as well as a quick get rich plan. Still, being a waiter was considered as a low or black person job. Black. In the case of private and country clubs, there was a sort of respect develop between the white member and the black waiter. There came a time when the member came to his favorite black waiter and asked if he would help do some work around the house. Over a period of time, the member's wife would need help in the house, so now the waiter's wife is working, making more money for the family. The family would soon be invited to picnics, holiday events, sport events, vacations, even fishing trips. Now suddenly, it's not so low of a job anymore. All whites weren't rich. Then it became necessary to study and shape and mold. What a server and service should be. Even so, what was considered the basic of both server and service no longer exist due to the advancement of society and so-called advance education. From what the waiter's uniform was, to how the food is served. Waiters were expected to wear white, cleaned, and ironed shirt, especially tuxedo shirts, ironed black slacks, white socks, and polished black, hard shoes. It was required to have In your possession, a pen, a pad to take an order, a side

I

towel to serve all courses of food, a crumbler to clean the crumbs, and a wine key. Most servers of today would not know what to do with a crumbler if they held it in their hands, nor when to use it. Presenting a bottle of wine, opening, serving, and knowledge of the basic of wine is a thing of the past. Before, you served soup on a saucer with a dolly on a dessert plate. Salads, no matter what dish (salad plate/bowl style) it came in, also was to be served on a dolly with a larger plate. Any entrée which came in a bowl, especially pasta, and dishes that were smaller than a normal entrée plate were served on an additional plate with a dolly. Tableside service is rare, and in most cases, not even heard of. Some say, "Tableside takes too long." Bullshit! You simply do not know what you are doing. As some dishes were required to be prepared tableside, it would take about the same time entrées from the kitchen were coming out. The combining of food coming out of the kitchen while entrée being prepared tableside would turn out together at the same time. There are many reasons tableside is no longer in existence, but the one which stands out the most, "You don't know how to do it," "You don't want to learn it," and end of subject. The side towel is used to serve each course, preventing your bare hands from touching the plate. Not to mention you want the customer to assume the plate was hot. As the one's who taught me, and myself, have had pride in being a waiter. We actually enjoyed the job of being a waiter. Teamwork at its best. Proud of the way we provided services to our table and enjoying the magic moments that we provided and the respect and appreciation the customer had showed and given. So far, I have given you a small insight to the history of being a waiter. So now let us talk about the service of a waiter.

Service of a Waiter

The individual. Since I am a male, I will be describing from a male point of view. Facial hair would not be permitted to serve food. Men with beards could never be hired to be a waiter or even around food. Your hair must be cut and neat in appearance. Your uniform said a lot about you, your demeanor, your character, and how you feel about your job, not to mention the customer. Clean white shirts neatly ironed. Cleaned and ironed black slacks. Black socks, no longer white, with polish, shined, hard style shoes. I had a saying that "I looked as good going to work as do some people's going out." Which bring us to the mental outlook of the waiter, directly, being a waiter is not for everybody. Many have tried for whatever personal reason there is and end up going from one place to another or quitting. It's never ceased to amaze me how an individual can work for a brief period of time is suddenly a professional waiter. LOL. I would say, "They can't be serious," but they really are. Tell them they are not professionals, and the fight is on. Some feel and think being a waiter is easy money. Who are you kidding? Far from it. Considering the truth of the matter, most would not want to serve themselves. Imagine coming to your table and seeing yourself (attitude) sitting there. Whew! What an ordeal that is going to be. Presentation is everything. The way you look, uniform, as well as body appearance, the way you greet the table, the table appearance, silverware, and glassware, and more importantly, knowledge of specials, the entire menu, food and drinks, even history of being a waiter.

As part of the founding of hospitality service, certain rules applied. One that stands out is when a couple would go out to eat at a restaurant, the waiter was considered a stranger and women were not allowed to talk to strangers in the days of old. While the waiter was getting their beverages, the gentleman would take the lady's order, and upon his return and readiness, give both orders to the waiter. I still do that style of service today. I especially like doing that with young couple and older couples who might remember those days. As I approach the table, the first thing you want to do is get a feel of the customer at the table. Consider this, you treat everyone the same by treating them differently to reach that one goal. Customer satisfaction. When you get assigned a table, they can see your name from your name tag as introduction, find out their last name and prefer to it when communicating with them. Speak their names at least three times during the course of the meal. Once at the greeting, during the course of the meal, and upon delivering the check. Overall, a warm, hearty welcome, a special heartfelt moment during the meal, and a heartfelt farewell. But back to the beginning! After you are assigned your station after doing line-up and all your priority has been accomplished, then you should check your table. Is everything you need on the table and is it in the proper place? The reason for the silverware to be placed as it is so it would be consistent, no matter where you go. The fork would go on the left because fork was spelled FORK and left was spelled LEFT. Same for the knife. RIGHT and KNIFE. You also set your silverware to be used from the outside in. same with your glassware. Your water glass is always the most used, so it will be the closest. White wine, red, then the champagne is last.

Setting Your Table!

As you approach your table, count the chairs around, assuring you have the proper amount. Stand behind the chair. Place the first fork just to the inside of the seat of the chair and at the tip edge of the table. Normally the coffee spoon is the utensil on the right, so you would position it just to the inside of the seat and tip edge of the table. Consider this, you should be able to draw an imaginary line from the first fork to the last spoon/soup spoon (RIGHT) and touch each utensil in between. Same things applied when you are setting round tables as well. Also, when the chairs are set around a round table with an odd number of chairs, no chair faces a chair on the other side. A practice I do is make a number one seat at each table. Go to the other side and place two chairs in a position where the number one seat divides them, then set the remaining chairs evenly around the table. No chair will face another. As you place the silverware at a round table, you can still imagine the imaginary line, keeping it within the boundaries of the seat. Your center piece should be center of the table. The island, salt and pepper and condiments should be placed where it is easily available to the customer. Butters and creamer should also have an assigned position on the table. This just came to me, the reason the blade of the knife points inward is because back in the times of old, one village would invite another village to feast. During the events of the evening at the right time, the inviting villager would pick up their knives, stretch out their hands, and stab and cut the other villagers. Some of the things I am telling you will not be found in a book or classroom, nor would an average waiter (wannabe) know, for it has only been passed down to the "real" waiters. There is so much more. Now moving along, your table is set, yourself is presentable to include tools, and your side work done, now you have a guest at your table.

Approaching the Table!

Over the years, I made a habit as I start to approach my table to find the order sheet, which should have their names; if not, ask the person seating the guest. If unknown, proceed to the table. Basically, if I know what time my tables come in, I will pre-set the water glass. As I stand at my table for a two top, between the couple but not so close, and four top between the two gentlemen. Good evening/afternoon, my name is Clarence and to whom do I have the pleasure of serving? Usually, once you have addressed the table, listen to everyone at the table. Respond to matters which are concerns to them. As you proceed in offering them a cocktail, a glass of wine, or another beverage of your choice, once I have set down the last ordered drink, which is always to the guest/person right, with my right hand, and always to the gentleman paying the bill. I suggest, "Everyone to enjoy your beverages and each other for a moment and I will return shortly with menus, and we will talk dinner or lunch." For lunch, you would bring menus when you approach the table, due to its fast pace. Often you might take their entrée order while taking their drink order. Time is the importance and/or they don't want to be disturbed at least as possible. Silent service Is the art of hand jesters to indicate your intension at the table. Up to this point, the service I have mentioned can be used for both lunch and dinner. Now I will be referring to dinner service from here on out. Now, even though you are giving them a moment, look back at the table to make sure it seems as if everyone is enjoying their drinks. After what should be considered "a moment," with specials and menus, proceed to the table. Announce your presence at the table, and with permission, to pass out the menus. Always start from the host right side, always with the eldest lady at the table, then the lady who has the kids, giving her their menus, too. If no kids, give all the other ladies and then the eldest gentleman (unless he is the host) down to the host. Should you have started from the host's right side, you should have given everyone their menus to their left side. Left side = give right side take, except all drinks are served on the right side.

After you have given the menu to the host, inform the table you have a few things of interest that you must tell them. Then you speak of the specials, how it is prepared, and are there any concerns about allergies and health concerns. Then you take the order in the same order as you pasted out the menus (Summary, at this point you should have successfully given a hearty, warm welcome, made them feel more relaxed, and expecting to have a wonderful evening. Keeping in mind you are going to attempt to make something unexpected to happen for as many and as often as you can for that table).

Serving the Course, One Course at a Time

Seat 1:   App, salad, entrée (Host)
Seat 2:   Soup, salad, entrée (Lady)
Seat 3:   Splitting app with seat 1, salad, entrée (Gentleman)
Seat 4:   Salad, entrée (Lady)

As you are beginning to put the order in the computer, first put in the app and send it to the kitchen to get it started, should it take time to prepare. Then type in the remaining orders. One way to share a magical moment is to have the kitchen split the app instead of having the guest do it themselves. In preparing your tray, you should get all four salads first, then app, and soup. Upon approaching the table, you would serve from the left: seat 2, soup, seat 4, salad, seat 3, then seat 1 app. Objective is to have everyone start eating at the same time. Once the apps and soup are done, serve seat 2, seat 3, then seat 1, their salad, leaving seat 4's dish on the table. As you present each course, always check back after a moment to make sure everything is ok, should there be a problem, you can attend to the situation in a timely manner. In some cases, a sorbet course may come before the main entrée. At this time, you would notify the chefs that you are ready for entrees. Clear from right, and if apply, serve the sorbet course.

Sorbet is served to cleanse your palate of the previous courses, leaving your mouth fresh to enjoy your meal. Nowadays, sorbet course is non-existent. But anyway, after notifying the cooks to bring up the entrees, then clear the table, and if clean, place the steak knife in its position and replace the entrée fork if it was used previously. Always replenish your water glasses, but from time to time, you might want to change those glasses if there is little to no ice in the original glass. Does that sound like a magical moment? Works for me! After serving the entrée, always check back to make sure all entrées will a require temperature is accordingly, as well as taste good! (Always when taking orders for beef, liver, ahi tuna will need to take a temperature) Just before you get ready to clear, check the table and ask if anyone would like a cup of coffee. If so, get it serving to the right of the person. When presenting the coffee, first place the cream and sugar bowl together on the table, announcing having done it, cream and sugar is on the table, serve the coffee. Clear the table! Present the desert display or menu. Again, replenish all refillable drinks as a way to up-sale and put more on the check. Flaming coffees was once considered as the after-dinner drinks, but again, is a thing of the past. Now that you have cleared the dessert dishes and no more coffee is desired, present the check to the host, while at the same time, addressing the entire table with a warm, heartfelt farewell. It is never easy to serve another, but it is a way service use to be and only in certain places today. Considering all I have mentioned should be as a basic of providing the best of the best service you can give.

Summary of What Service and Server Might Be!

First and foremost is the presentation and mindset of the waiter. I have always been a huge fan of ironing. I do not do permanent press; they don't look ironed. My shoes have to shine like a newly pressed penny. That's for real shiny. Considering the beauty of my living, presentation is necessary. Shower, bath, haircut. Putting all this together, I am ready for work. Only according to where you work, what personal tools you will need to do your job. For lunch you will need a pen, pad, and side towel. You must know what is available other than what is on the menu. Specials, and if added buffet, buffet items. Time is a factor and therefor, must be taken into consideration. In private clubs, you want to call the members by name at least three times during the meal. Also, should you prefer to their guest by their name, at least three things will happen. 1) the guest will think highly of the member belonging to the club such as this, 2) a subconscious thought that he could be a member here, and 3) the waiter and service is exceptionally good, if not WONDERFUL. In private clubs, "members' satisfaction is the ultimate goal, the only goal. In some clubs, members come in for lunch on a regular and may have a special concern, you should identify what they are in your presentation at the table. In the present of a guest, it will truly be a conversation piece with guaranteed results.

Dinner is more laid back but more complicated than lunch. Your uniform might be different from lunch to dinner. Nevertheless, your uniform must be clean and hopefully ironed, and your hard sole shoes are polished and shined. You should at least have knowledge of the regular menu items, the mixture of drinks, and a fair amount of knowledge concerning wines. As a waiter, you must consider some of your guests have worked somewhere and haven't stopped moving since they got off from work, and now it's their time to unwind. You treat everyone the same by treating them differently. Acknowledging this advice will help you in providing quality service. Every individual deserves the best of your service, regardless of the picture looking from the outside in. Good evening, name recognition with a smile, warm heartedly, usually puts a pause on the individual thoughts to at least acknowledge you back and possibly with a smile.

Let us Do Dinner!

Since I began in the hospitality business being a waiter, I have mainly worked formal fine dining, so everything will be of that scenario. Also, vision being in a respected restaurant or private club. No matter where you work, if you must take an order from a table can benefit from something I've mentioned. First of all, prepare yourself, mentally, to be at work. Do you really want to be at work today? If so, what degree or depth of service will you render? What standards do you hold highest amongst your co-workers, as well with the management? How much do you prep preparing to work! Do you wait to be told? Or are you asked to be told? Does it matter if it seems you might be doing sometimes all the side work? In my case, not at all. I take that opportunity to set things up like it is supposed to be and show the way things are supposed to look when it is done. Then when others take the responsibility, it will always be the same. Always check your table to suit you and your professionalism. Trust no one as to how your tables look. No matter how busy you are, there will always be time to check your table and adjust them to your satisfaction. Sometimes when you have a specific table, their may come a time when something extra may be needed as a request granted for that table. "Never get caught with your pants down!" Presentation and being prepared equals knowledge, goes hand-in-hand. Now your table is set. One more thing I do is check the menus, should they be preset or presented at the table to include a wine list, for cleanliness, and having the right menu enclosed. Before approaching any table, arm yourself with knowledge. Look again and pick out at least two items that you personally like from each category and are able to describe but know something about everything. Especially if a situation arrives, you might need to substitute a standard item due to a health issue. Consider items that may also help to up-sale your check. Also know as many varieties of wine as possible. By name, by origin, by content, as well as how to describe how to view the wine in the glass during the tasting of the wine. Do not forget your physical tools, your pens, one to write with, one for member to sign their check, and extra spare, a pad to take an order, a crumbler to keep your table clean at all times, a wine key to open their choice of wine, and a side towel to handle the dishes that is being served. I also prefer to my side towel as a splash guard when refilling beverages and an extra napkin when needed. Back in the days of old, you were also required to have a black lighter should a member need a light for his cigarette while sitting at the table. Then take one more look at yourself and think about what you are going to do, how you are going to do it, to what the aim, outcome, when it's done! Now! Let us bring on the tables. There is nothing nor no one who can dictate the event of the evening you will experience, just make sure the experience is a good one! From what I have provided you with, hopefully, will give you a better outlook at the wonderful life of being a waiter. It is never easy pleasing and serving another, but in a lot of time, it really is. Again, to what degree or depth you take being a waiter can be rewarding in more ways than you can imagine. There is not a day that goes by I haven't wanted to go to work. I love my work, how I look, the impression I characterize, where I work, and to whom I work with. Those, too, can be a key factor in your decision to succeed as a waiter. Though you can take all that I have attempted to make known, still, being a waiter is not for everybody. Only you know for sure! You will know, your co-workers as well as your manager will also know you, after a while. A waiter's job deserves the best person to do it as any professional career job. Hospitality is a professional business in which quality work is by quality patrons.

A Real Waiter, Old School Style

It is not always about the money on the check or on the table. You are going to do that anyway. Every table has a subconscious mind on how much they want to spend, yet the tip is yours to get, determines your level of service. A top of knowing the job and the operations, waiter in his services. It is a must. You, as I do, should make a continuous statement as to the style waiter you are. Often an individual starts out attempting to make an impression, only to fade by the way and never wants to do no more than that one job when they want to do that one job. A real waiter has no boundaries. There is nothing that won't be attempted and completed successfully. He/she is the one that the managers go to when a special project needs particular care or a special guest requires special attention. An ideal waiter is someone whom you do not see and can be found working, cleaning a particular area, or setting up for usage later or even for another day. Most real waiters find things to do while there is time. Often, they are the one who gets everyone else going doing something. If there is a special table or cart that must be set up, they are the ones to set it up to the point that they insist on setting it up! Not to mention there are other servers who can walk in a dining room and point out the table that you set, no matter how many tables are in the room. As an individual, as a waiter, there is no one else who can be you, so why not be the best that other sees. When approaching your table, bring with your confidence, appearance, personal character, and a broad knowledge of foods, wines, and even how long the place has been in operation. Dedicated waiters can be spotted across the room. Often, other tables will start to watch you, just to see what you will do next.

At the Table!

As your guests approach the table, standing off to the side, allow everyone to choose their seats, immediately move to the lady chair, pulling it out and taking her napkin. Seat her by pushing her chair under her, coming to her right side, facing her, and lay the napkin in her lap. By doing this, I always state your waiter is a gentleman. Afterward, and after giving your representation, this would be the perfect time to use the "woman as a stranger" routine and go from there. You may get by only knowing a little about foods, but it is sometimes more beneficial to know about wines. Some guests may not have a cocktail but a glass of wine instead. If at least three people are having the same flavor of wine, insist they purchase a bottle. Should they purchase a bottle of white wine, present a wine bucket, containing ice and some water to the right of the host. If not, the person ordering the wine. Set the glasses, white for whites, red for reds. From the right side of the ordering guest, present the wine with the label facing the guest, assuring the guest of his selection. The label should never turn from the guest's face. Just pour a small amount for taste. Before pouring for the taste, in the case of white wine, place the cork on the right of the guest on the table. In the case of red wine, you present the cork to the guest. Most guests want to smell it or squeeze it or both. The next thing that happens has several meanings. In testing the taste of the red wine, the guest swirls the wine in the glass, holds the glass up, and watches it. Back in the days of old, after the wine stopped swirling in the glass, the object was to watch the lines (refer to as legs) return to the wine. The longer it takes, the better the quality of the wine.

When taste testing the wine, you let the wine flow from the tip of the tongue to the middle, to the back, and then swallow. Most people have surpassed this technique, but it is nice to know history. Also having a knowledge of the content and origin of the wine you are serving, can be a plus. The different ingredients, the type of container its stored in, even the process of storing and ageing of the wine. When preparing to clear, ask your guest about coffee service. If so, serve it first, then clear the dishes and crumb your table. Present dessert display (menu), take order, offer after dinner drinks as an up-sale and a good ideal for the guest. Serve your dessert and refresh their coffees and other refillable beverages. Upon clearing your dessert dishes and the request for more beverages is denied, present the check to the host, and give your heartfelt farewell.

Consider Doing This!

As all females approach your table, make the effort to seat them and place their napkins over their lap. In the case of a man, you place his napkin over his right leg.

Yes, sir, no, sir. Yes ma! No ma!

Serve always, from the left, except all beverages are served from the right, and you also clear from the right. You will also crumb from the right.

When refilling beverages on the table, use your side towel as a splash guard.

Use your side towel when serving all courses. Never serve dishes in bowls smaller than an entrée plate directly on the table. Serve on a dolly on a larger plate.

After you have served each course , give the guest a moment, then check back to make sure it is to their pleasing. If not, be a problem solver.

Have patience with the children. Put their order in first and serve them immediately.

Should your place of business have pepper shakers, you should, no, you must always offer fresh ground pepper with all salads and pasta dishes. Actually, it's a custom.

When serving alcohol beverages, as you present a beverage that differ from the first, state to the individual that it is a custom; after presenting the second drink that I remove the fist one, may I do that at this time? Whether yes or no, you displayed knowledge and attempt to up-keep your table.

Always while the guest is standing when served a beverage, it is to be served with a napkin.

When an individual has been seated and has a base plate at his position, place the napkin in the base plate and drink on top of it.

When time to serve a course, from the right side, place the beverage at the top of the individual place setting and take the napkin away.

No base plate, place beverage directly in front of individual with no napkins. You do not put paper on cloth.

As you serve a course, remove the utensil of the previous course.

In a course where you supply the utensil, fork on left, knives, knives and spoons or soup spoon on the right on the table.

In the case where certain individuals order more than one course, I serve each person their first course. As each guest finishes their first course, serve their second course, leaving the dish for the person having only one course before the entrée. Once all the second courses have been , and completed, clear everyone together (Serving the eldest lady first and so forth should never be spoken, it is automatic).

In all courses, state what it is you are serving and temperature when it applies.

Remember, treat each person the same by treating them differently.

For wine service, use the designated glass for the wine that is served.

Present the glasses and wine bucket in the case of white wine.

Also, feel free to exchange your guest's water glass if it is not presentable, especially if it has no ice.

Occasionally, you may need to give a guest a fresh napkin if theirs is stained. Without saying a word just change their napkin with a new one.

After receiving the food order, it might be necessary to use "silent service." Hand gestures will be your way of communicating your intents. Also, with silent service, you need only walk around the table, making eye contact with each person. If something is wrong, they will let you know.

Provide everything necessary to complete the guest meal. Baked potatoes, burgers, sandwiches may require certain condiments, provide them without question.

Be aware of your table. Read your table as to being ready to proceed with the event of the evening.

Time is of the essence, use it wisely. Do not waste unnecessary time with slow service, but they're not cattle either.

Know your temperatures. Make sure you take a temperature for all beef entrée, tuna entrée, liver entrée, and even salmon entrée.

Always present yourself as a knowledgeable, well-presentable, professional waiter.

Last, but truly most important, let your present be known. If you come up behind someone and they do not know you are there, "I'm behind you," "Coming in/out" through doorways but say something.

Maintain a good relationship with the kitchen.

Maintain a good relationship with your co-workers as well as management personal.

Be someone others look up to and respect as a waiter an individual.

Serving Bottles of Wine

After receiving the order, preset proper wine glass, and in the case of white wine, preset wine bucket (iced water) next to person who ordered wine.

Present wine with label facing individual, describing the wine chosen by name and origin.

Open the bottle without turning label from guest view.

For white wines, you place the cork on the table; for red wines, you present the cork to the individual.

Pour a small amount (in either case, red or white) for taste.

Upon approval, proceed to the eldest lady pouring her glass, then the other ladies, from the oldest gentleman to the host (With the proper glass, you pour until the wine is going up in the glass) (In the days of old, everyone would have a taste of the wine for their approval before pouring).

After the wine is served to each person, place red wine bottle in front of host or in the wine (white) bucket. Each bottle can serve four glasses evenly. After pouring wine, check with host to see if a back-up is necessary or a different wine will be served later. If so, gather the necessary glasses, placing them to the side until needed.

If no more wine is to be served, unless told to remove empty bottle, place red wine bottle in front of host (or person doing ordering or in the wine bucket for whites). Also, after returning white wine to bucket, wrap a napkin around the neck of the bottle. As you refill the glasses, you will use napkin to wipe the bottle as you take it out the bucket upon clearing your table of the red wine bottle from the table, and the wine bucket as well, leaving the cork on the table. Once you have served dessert dishes, upon clearing, then you remove the corks. Keep in mind, once you have cleared your entrée course, there shouldn't be anything on the table except glassware, water glasses, and wine glasses (if there is wine still left in glasses, if not, remove them). If during the meal someone should request a glass of iced tea, then you would place the sugar bowl on the table; if not, there is no need to have it on the table. Lunch service, you must have it on the table.

When Serving Coffee Service

Usually some will pour the coffee in the cup while still in the kitchen and then proceed to the table and serve. Though it may seem to save the person time, it does nothing for the coffee, and once cream is added, the coffee is lukewarm at best. Waiters serves the cup at the table and then pour the coffee in the cup. That is a better service. But then I, on the other hand, before I leave the kitchen, on my tray is the proper amount of coffee cups, all filled with the hottest water I can find, with an empty glass, saucers, cream in a creamer, and sugar bowl on the table for all to see. I place the saucer in front of individual, pick up the water, fill the cup over the tray, swirl the water in the cup, not spilling it over the side, pour water into empty glass, set it on saucer, and pour coffee. This is one of my personal signatures served "magic moment."

Your Table

The most crucial factor between the guest and the waiter is the table. The guest to which they will dine, and the waiter to whom it belongs. Presentation, presentation, presentation! Consider this, you want the host to be impressed that his guests may also be impressed of the host, the waiter, and possibly the establishment. Not only are you a waiter, but you are also a salesperson. Often the appearance of the table has a way of giving a thought, in the guest's mind, how the evening might go, especially after you have greeted the table. No matter how much or how little is on the table, the presentation of the table should always be its best, regardless, and continuously. You can set a thousand place setting and every one of them looks like the first one. Skills of that nature takes pride (As I say, being a waiter only requires the best person for the job. This is a profession).

When placing your silverware, keep everything inside the seat of the chair in which an individual will be seating. Place your silverware no more than one-eighth of an inch from the edge. Draw an imaginary line from the first fork to the last spoon and assure all utensils touches that line in between. Here are some pictures of various places settings you may need to set (Nevertheless, many establishments have their own way of setting, but in any case, you eat from the outside in, no matter what the establishment).

This procedure is done when the table is preset, and dessert utensils are at the top of the setting. Regardless of whether there is either a fork or spoon or both, as you clear the entrée dish, bread and butter plate, and used utensils, dishes in your left hand, take your right hand, with class, move fork to the left position, and/or the spoon to the right position. This also shows true profession of the waiter. Your detail to the table is never ending.

Clearing

First, you always, always clear from the guest's right-hand side with your right hand. Never clear with your left hand or/and the guest's left side with your right hand. As if you are standing between the guests. Keeping your table cleaned is necessary for real waiters. If possible, beverage napkins should never lay on a cloth table or any paper.

Clear cocktail glasses, when presenting another cocktail whether the same as the first one or another, such as a glass of wine. When you clear courses, clear everything that goes with that course.

When you clear the entrée course, upon clearing the entrée dish, also at the same time, clear all bread-and-butter plates with the butter knife, salt and pepper shaker, leaving sugar bowl if it was on the table and breadbasket is no longer needed. Only utensil that left on the table is the coffee spoon. This is also the best time to crumb your table. Often when clearing the salad course, there may be bites of lettuce and breadcrumbs on the table. If you should never put a dirty dish on a tray with clean dishes, then why would you put an entrée on a dirty table. Um. Unless it is the same bottle of wine as the first, then you don't pour new wine into old glasses, even if it's the same kind but a different name. Always present and preset clean glasses, and after pouring new wine, attempt to remove the previous glass. Maintenance should never take second hand to time. Always be prepared.

Changing the Linens

I have been to my share of different restaurants, and as a waiter, I watch other waiters. And one thing I can say is the changing of the tablecloth has faded by the wayside. Me being me, I ask some of them, have you ever heard of changing the tablecloth without showing the top of the table. Have you? Their answer, like yours, was no! Well then, this is how you do it!

Lunch time (during this illustration, consider there are people in the dining room).

In most cases, after you have cleared your table of its dishes, there should only be the island left on the table (Salt and pepper shaker and sugar bowl). Move those things to one side of the table, close to the edge. Proceed to the opposite side, fold the hanging tablecloth to where it just lays over the edge of the table. Move back to the beginning with your new tablecloth. Without fully opening it, unfold the tablecloth halfway with the seam down. Stretch out the tablecloth, pass the table into the chair on the other side. Holding the new tablecloth by its edge, reach down, grabbing the old tablecloth and pull it towards you. Stop, take the island (S&P, sugar bowl), and place on the new cloth. Continue to pull the two cloths until the old one is in your hands. Straighten the island and set the table. Should you leave the island on the table or move it to another table, etc. but NEVER sit the island in the seat of a chair. You never put anything where you put your ASS! Really!

For dinner time, it is the same procedure, except there shouldn't be anything on the table. No guest should see the tabletop. In some cases, the table might be long. If you can reach across the table, you can walk down the side of the table and still not show the top of the table. The illustration shows a dinner time/extended table changing of the tablecloth.

Just for Fun!

Here are two salads you can prepare at home to impress your guest, friends, or family. The Gingham salad is a simple, refreshing, and satisfying salad or entrée should you add chicken breast, some shrimps, or even some salmon. The Caesar salad recipe is the bomb. Should you follow that recipe as told, it will be the best Caesar that you can make, unless I personally made it. But, by all means, enjoy yourself and others to enjoy you!

Gingham Salad

This salad has no certain quantity of ingredient to measure by you merely make this salad according to taste and amount of people served.

In a large bowl, add:

Spinach leaves
Fr. Raspberries
Fr. Blueberries
Fr. Blackberries
Sliced almonds (preferred toasted)
Fr. Sliced strawberries

Mix all the above ingredients together. Just before it is time for salads, add a raspberry-poppy seed vinaigrette to the salad, then serve it.

Enjoy! Opal

Tableside Caesar's Salad (for 4)

Recipe!

Caesar's salad bowl
Anchovies
Garlic
Parmesan cheese (grated)
Lemon juice from a ½ lemon
Egg in a soup cup w/hot water
Dijon mustard
Oil
Vinegar (red wine)
Romaine lettuce
Croutons
Fresh ground pepper

Using two serving spoons in a Caesar's salad bowl, grind four turn of fresh ground black pepper. Take four anchovies and crush into a bowl. Add garlic. Squeeze half lemon juice into bowl. Crack egg and add only the yolk to mixture, stirring the mixtures together. Add Dijon mustard. Mix one spoon of red wine vinegar. Add three spoons of oil and stir into mixture. Add a healthy amount of parmesan cheese, stirring into mixture. Add romaine and croutons, stirring mixing all mixture together. Spoon into salad bowl. Spoon more par cheese and add two anchovies atop. Serve.

Some places will start putting the lettuce in the bowl first. I do not feel by doing this you are able to fully mix all the ingredients together. Understand, after you add the lemon juice, then the egg yolk, the lemon juice cooks the egg yolk, the Dijon mustard stops the cooking. The ratio of vinegar and oil is one spoonful of vinegar not running to three spoons running of oil. The spoon is a serving spoon. When adding garlic and mustard, use the tip of the spoon to add the ingredient. I normally can tell by the smell if I have prepared my Caesar salad correctly. Also, you put the egg in a soup cup of hot water, so it will be easy to separate the yolk from the egg white when adding to mixture (In the beginning, you put one anchovy per person at the table having the salad).

Last Page!

Enclosing! I should stop here and I'm going to. From the information I have provided, even if you never waited a table in your life, you will be fine. The business of being a waiter deserves the best person for the job, like any other profession. Be the best you can be, no matter what you do. I personally love my job and how I go about doing it. I respect my co-workers, management, and most importantly, the people in which I serve. So, to whomever reads this book, I pray that it be uplifting and can help improve the service you are providing. There is no situation that can be described that you will face, but as a professional, there's no situation you can't face with success at the end of the ordeal.

About the Author

I, Clarence E. Palmer Sr., am a server of people! On Earth and until heaven. I have always tried to help another. There was something about a sharp dressed waiter. Not to mention how they did their job! I liked it from the first time I saw them to the point I had to be one. So, I did, and thanks to the "old school" waiter, I was educated through education. I will never forget my first "on-my-own" tableside. It was a Steak Diane followed by a Banana Foster for two. That was one of my most memorable nights ever. Being a waiter to me is as serious as being a doctor is to him or her. Much of the old school style of service in these days and time no longer exist. But for all of those "old schools" whom are still in the business, there are some things we just cannot stop doing. This book is to tell of the way we used to be. Secrets will be shared and days of old will be relived. This is our way, the old school way in the professionalism of being a waiter. Enjoy! Opal.

I would truly be wrong if I do not give credit to the one whom suggested I should be a waiter. Thank you, Mr. Michael Taylor, a.k.a. "Mike Mike." Also, to Mr. Robert Haynes, my teacher of the tableside service.